THE
PURPOSE
OF
Christmas

STUDY GUIDE

RICK WARREN

THE
PURPOSE
OF
Christmas

A THREE-SESSION STUDY
FOR GROUPS AND FAMILIES

STUDY GUIDE

 HarperChristian
Resources

SaddlebackResources.com

The Purpose of Christmas Study Guide
Copyright © 2008 by Rick Warren

Requests for information should be addressed to:
HarperChristian Resources, 3900 Sparks Dr. SE, Grand Rapids, Michigan 49546

ISBN 978-0-310-31855-2

Interior design by Christine Orejuela-Winkelman

Printed in the United States of America

ONTENTS

UNDERSTANDING YOUR STUDY GUIDE

Here is a brief explanation of the features of this study guide.

Looking Ahead/Catching Up: You will open each meeting with an opportunity for everyone to check in with each other about how you are doing with the weekly assignments. Accountability is a key to success in this study!

Key Verse: Each week you will find a key verse or Scripture passage for your group to read together. If someone in the group has a different translation, ask them to read it aloud so the group can get a bigger picture of the meaning of the passage.

Video Lesson: There is a fifteen-minute video lesson for the group to watch together each week. Fill in the blanks in the lesson outline as you watch the video, and be sure to refer back to this outline during your discussion time.

Discovery Questions: Each video segment is complemented by several questions for group discussion. Please don't feel pressured to discuss every single question. The material in this study is meant to be your servant, not your master. So there is no reason to rush through it. Give everyone ample opportunity to share their thoughts. If you don't get through all of the discovery questions, that's okay.

Living on Purpose: In his book, *The Purpose Driven® Life*, Rick Warren identifies God's five purposes for our lives: worship, fellowship, discipleship, ministry, and evangelism. We will focus on one of these five purposes in each lesson, and discuss how it relates to the subject of the study. This section is very important, so please be sure to leave time for it.

Putting It into Practice: This is where the rubber meets the road. We don't want to be just hearers of the Word; we also need to be doers of the Word (James 1:22). This section of the study explains the assignments we would like you to complete before your next meeting. These assignments are application exercises that will help you put into practice the truths you have discussed in the lesson.

Prayer Direction: There are two parts to this feature, one for personal prayer and one for group prayer requests. In the Personal Prayer section, we have given you prompts to help focus your prayer. Take a moment to write a personal prayer based on what you learned in the session and what you're most thankful for. Then invite the group to share their prayer requests and write them in the Group Prayer section. Close your meeting by praying for one another's requests. Praying together is one of the greatest privileges of small group life. Don't take it for granted.

Daily Christmas Prayer Journal: At the end of each lesson we have added two pages for a Daily Christmas Prayer Journal. This journal is uniquely designed to help you record your thoughts and reflections to God on a daily basis. You will find simple suggestions to help get you started each day in a conversation with God. This feature is perfect for those who are not accustomed to journaling. Discover the beauty of the Christmas season and a deeper connection with God by completing your Daily Christmas Prayer Journal.

Host Tips: These brief instructions highlighted in shaded boxes throughout the study guide are helpful coaching hints for your group host. Here's your first tip:

> **HOST TIP:** The study guide material is meant to be your servant, not your master. The point is not to race through the sessions; the point is to take time to let God work in your lives. Nor is it necessary to "go around the circle" before you move on to the next question. Give people freedom to speak, but don't insist that they do. Your group will enjoy deeper, more open sharing and discussion if people don't feel pressured to speak up.

How to Use This Video Curriculum

Follow these simple steps for a successful discussion time:

1. Open your meeting by using the Looking Ahead or Catching Up section of your study guide.
2. Watch the video lesson together and follow along in the outline in this study guide. Each video lesson is about fifteen minutes long.
3. Discuss the Discovery Questions, Living on Purpose, and Putting It into Practice assignments.
4. Close your session by following the Prayer Direction instructions.

It's just that easy! Have a great discussion time.

The Purpose of Christmas Book

To maximize the impact of this study, we recommend that each participant have a copy of this study guide and the book *The Purpose of Christmas*. Reading assignments and in-group review of *The Purpose of Christmas* are a vital part of this learning experience. The book will become a valuable, permanent resource for review and sharing once you have completed this study.

SESSION ONE

A Time for Celebration

> **HOST TIP:** Welcome! If you are doing this study with a small group, give everyone a chance to introduce themselves and briefly share how they came to be a part of the group. Then take a few minutes to review the Group Guidelines on pages 57–58. These guidelines will help everyone know what to expect and how to contribute to a meaningful small group time.

LOOKING AHEAD

1. Briefly share your favorite Christmas memory.

2. Is anything distracting you from the joy of this season?

KEY VERSE

For God so loved the world that he gave his one and only Son,
that whoever believes in him shall not perish but have eternal life.

John 3:16 NIV

Watch the Session One video now and fill in the blanks in the outline on pages 13–15. Refer back to the outline during your discussion time.

$\mathcal{A}$ Time for Celebration

The birth of Jesus Christ is the most significant event in the history of mankind. It split history into BC and AD. Every time you write a check, celebrate a birthday, fill out an application form, or any time you use a date, you're using the birth of Jesus Christ as the basis for measuring time.

Christmas was God's idea. He planned when it would happen, how it would happen, where it would happen, and why it would happen. And since it was his idea, we should find out what he had in mind.

On the night Jesus Christ was born, God sent an angel to announce his arrival. In that birth announcement, we find God's three purposes of Christmas.

> *[8]And there were shepherds living out in the fields nearby, keeping watch over their flocks at night. [9]An angel of the Lord appeared to them, and the glory of the Lord shone around them, and they were terrified. [10]But the angel said to them, "Do not be afraid. I bring you good news of great joy that will be for all the people." (Luke 2:8 – 10 NIV)*

The first purpose of Christmas is _____.

Three Reasons to Celebrate

1. God _____ you.

> *"God so loved the world that he gave his one and only Son, that whoever believes in him shall not perish but have eternal life." (John 3:16 NIV)*

What God is saying to you at Christmas is, "I love you. It's not just the *world* I love — it's *you* that I love." God's love isn't based on what you do. His love is based on who he is.

> [35]*Can anything ever separate us from Christ's love? Does it mean he no longer loves us if we have trouble or calamity, or are persecuted, or hungry, or destitute, or in danger, or threatened with death?...* [37]*No, despite all these things, overwhelming victory is ours through Christ, who loved us.* [38]*And I am convinced that nothing can ever separate us from God's love. Neither death nor life, neither angels nor demons, neither our fears for today nor our worries about tomorrow — not even the powers of hell can separate us from God's love.* [39]*No power in the sky above or in the earth below — indeed, nothing in all creation will ever be able to separate us from the love of God that is revealed in Christ Jesus our Lord. (Romans 8:35 – 39 NLT)*

2. God is _____ **you.**

> [7]*Where can I go from your Spirit? Where can I flee from your presence?* [8]*If I go up to the heavens, you are there; if I make my bed in the depths, you are there.* [9]*If I rise on the wings of the dawn, if I settle on the far side of the sea,* [10]*even there your hand will guide me, your right hand will hold me fast. (Psalm 139:7 – 10 NIV)*
>
> *"I will never leave you; I will never abandon you." (Hebrews 13:5 TEV)*

God will never abandon you. You may not feel like he's near, but that just means you're not tuned in. You're not connected. You're not plugged into the source.

> *"It is not good for the man to be alone." (Genesis 2:18 NIV)*
>
> *God sets the lonely in families. (Psalm 68:6 NIV)*

3. God is _____ **you.**

God is not against you. He's not out to get you or make you miserable. He's on your side. He wants to give your life purpose and meaning.

> *"God did not send his Son into the world to condemn it, but to save it." (John 3:17 LB)*
>
> *If God is for us, who can be against us? (Romans 8:31 NIV)*

The God who created the universe, and who set the stars in their places and the world on its axis, says, "I love you, I am with you, I am for you." No matter who you are, where you've come from, or what you've done in your life, the Good News is for you. And that is worth celebrating!

DISCOVERY QUESTIONS

1. Which of the following statements is the most meaningful to you in this season of your life and why? God loves you. God is with you. God is for you.

2. Read Romans 8:35 – 39 in the outline (see page 14) and underline the phrase that means the most to you. Briefly explain why you selected that phrase.

3. Psalm 68:6 says, *"God sets the lonely in families."* How has God used your family, friends, or even this group to help you experience his love?

4. If you really believe God is for you and not against you, what is one thought, attitude, or behavior that you need to change?

5. Now that you know how much God loves you, how will that affect the way you celebrate Christmas this year?

LIVING ON PURPOSE: FELLOWSHIP

Do you have a friend or family member who needs to hear the truths you learned today? Why not invite them to join your group? Turn to the Circles of Life diagram on page 59 of this study guide. Take a moment to ask God to bring to your mind the names of people for each category in the diagram. Then commit to your small group that you will invite at least one person from your Circles of Life diagram to your next group meeting. Prepare for growth! Surveys have found that at least half of those invited to a small group accept the invitation.

PUTTING IT INTO PRACTICE

1. *The Purpose of Christmas,* by Rick Warren, is the perfect complement to this DVD study. Read pages 3 – 37 this week. Be prepared to share your thoughts and insights with the group in your next session.

2. It's party time! Pastor Rick challenged your group to host a simple Christmas party for your friends, family, neighbors, and coworkers. What's important right now is to decide who is going to host it and when you are going to have it. The best person to host the party is usually the most outgoing person in your group. But everybody has to get involved by bringing something and inviting someone. This could be a cookie exchange, a potluck, a night of caroling, etc. Take a moment to write down the names of a couple people you could invite, and then discuss plans with your group.

_____   _____

PRAYER DIRECTION

> **HOST TIP:** If your group has more than seven or eight people, you may want to break into smaller groups for prayer.

Following you will find two sections, one for personal prayer and one for group prayer requests. Take a few minutes to write a personal prayer based on today's session and what you're most thankful about. Then write down a few of the group prayer requests before you pray together.

Sometimes talking to God can be scary, but nothing can be scarier than being asked to pray out loud. After personal and group prayer requests are made you may want to have people pray, "Lord I thank you

for _____ . God I need help with _____ .
Jesus, I'm trusting you with _____ ."
This may help everyone get started.

Personal Prayer

Father, today I learned ... _____

_____

_____

_____

_____

_____

Thank you, Lord, for ... _____

_____

_____

_____

_____

_____

Group Prayer

Name   Request

_____   _____

_____   _____

_____   _____

_____   _____

_____   _____

_____   _____

_____   _____

_____   _____

DAILY CHRISTMAS PRAYER JOURNAL

God desires to have a relationship with you where you connect with him throughout the day. This comes naturally for some people, but for others this is not so easy. That's why we have created this Daily Christmas Prayer Journal where you can write your daily conversations with God.

This journal is uniquely designed to help you record your thoughts and reflections to God on a daily basis. You will find simple suggestions to help get you started each day in a conversation with God. This journal is perfect for those who are not accustomed to journaling. For those who are, it's like your own daily Advent journal. Discover the beauty of the Christmas season and a deeper connection with God by completing your Daily Christmas Prayer Journal.

Now turn the page to begin your Daily Christmas Prayer Journal.

DAILY CHRISTMAS PRAYER JOURNAL

Dear God, this Christmas I hope ...   *December 1*

_____

_____

_____

_____

Lord, I am so grateful ...   *December 2*

_____

_____

_____

_____

_____

Father, help me see ...   *December 3*

_____

_____

_____

_____

_____

Lord, help me celebrate ...   *December 4*

_____

_____

_____

_____

Forgive me, Lord, for ...   *December 5*

_____

_____

_____

_____

Father, I pray for ...   *December 6*

_____

_____

_____

_____

Lord, help my family to see ...   *December 7*

_____

_____

_____

_____

SESSION TWO
A Time for Salvation

CATCHING UP

1. If you read the assigned pages (3 – 37) in *The Purpose of Christmas* this week, share something that was particularly meaningful to you.

2. In our last session, we learned that God loves you, he is with you, and he is for you. What is one thought, idea, or Scripture passage that has helped you apply any of these truths?

KEY VERSE

It is by grace you have been saved, through faith — and this not from yourselves, it is the gift of God — not by works, so that no one can boast.

Ephesians 2:8–9 NIV

Watch the Session Two video now and fill in the blanks in the outline on pages 25 – 27. Refer back to the outline during your discussion time.

$\mathcal{A}$ Time for Salvation

The first purpose of Christmas is celebration. The second purpose of Christmas can be found in the very next statement the angel made:

Today in the city of David there has been born for you a Savior, who is Christ the Lord. (Luke 2:11 NASB)

The second purpose of Christmas is _____.

Surveys have confirmed that 90 percent of our society prays on a regular basis. What that means is that people recognize their need for somebody greater than themselves — someone to help them through a problem, rescue them from a tight spot, and ultimately save them from something they can't solve on their own.

Three Dimensions of Salvation

Salvation is three-dimensional. You are saved *from* something, you are saved *for* something, and you are saved *by* something.

1. Jesus came to save you *from* _____.

Sin is an attitude. It's a pride problem. Sin is saying, "I want to be my own boss. I don't need God."

For everyone has sinned; we all fall short of God's glorious standard. (Romans 3:23 NLT)

The problem with sin is that it separates us from God.

Your sins are the roadblock between you and your God. That's why he doesn't answer your prayers. (Isaiah 59:2 CEV)

Jesus came to set you free from your sin. But there's something else you need to be set free from. You need to be set free from yourself.

> *[24]I've tried everything, and nothing helps. I'm at the end of my rope. Is there no one who can do anything for me?... [25]The answer, thank God, is that Jesus Christ can and does. (Romans 7:24–25 MSG)*

The answer to your problem is not in a place, a program, or a pill. It's not jumping into another relationship. The answer to your sin problem and to your dissatisfaction in life is Jesus Christ. You need a Savior.

2. Jesus came to save you *for* a _____.

> *[God] saved us and called us to be his own people, not because of what we have done, but because of his own purpose and grace. (2 Timothy 1:9 TEV)*
>
> *It's in Christ that we find out who we are and what we are living for. Long before we first heard of Christ and got our hopes up, he had his eye on us, had designs on us for glorious living, part of the overall purpose he is working out in everything and everyone. (Ephesians 1:11–12 MSG)*

God has a plan and a purpose for your life. He's had it all along. As your Creator, he knows what's best for you. He not only saves you from your sins, but he saves you for a purpose — a purpose he wants you to fulfill. You will never be completely satisfied until you find out what that purpose is and how to bring it to pass.

You can live life at one of three levels: the survival level, the success level, or the significance level. You were made for significance. Significance comes from knowing God, knowing his purpose for your life, and then doing it.

You were made by God and for God, and until you understand that, life is never going to make sense.

3. Jesus came to save you *by* his _____.

What is grace? Grace is when God gives you what you need and not what you deserve. Grace is when God says, "I'm going to take your problem and make it my problem."

G _____

R _____

A _____

C _____

E _____

It is by grace you have been saved, through faith — and this not from yourselves, it is the gift of God — not by works, so that no one can boast. (Ephesians 2:8–9 NIV)

The Good News is this: Jesus Christ came to save you. He came to save you *from* your hurts, your habits, and your hang-ups. He came to save you *for* his purpose, and *by* his grace.

DISCOVERY QUESTIONS

1. You are saved *from* your sins, *for* God's purpose, and *by* his grace. Which of those three truths speaks loudest to you today?

2. What does it mean to you that your sins are forgiven? How did you first experience Christ's forgiveness in your life?

3. Pastor Rick talked about living at three levels: survival, success, and significance. What could you do between now and your next session to help you discover God's greater purpose in your life?

4. Read Ephesians 2:8 and Matthew 5:16. If God saves us by his grace and not by our works, then why are "good works" important?

5. The angel said, *"There has been born for you a Savior, who is Christ the Lord"* (Luke 2:11 NASB). Why did our Savior have to be born? Why couldn't he just come down from the sky or miraculously appear?

LIVING ON PURPOSE: MINISTRY

It can be difficult to turn good intentions into reality. It takes foresight and planning to live our lives on purpose. That's why we're encouraging each person to plan a simple Christmas project in your neighborhood with your family or friends — something to reach out to others in need. It could be making a Christmas meal for a needy family or a shut-in, Christmas caroling at a convalescent home, handing out cookies on your street, serving at a soup kitchen, purchasing Christmas gifts for children, etc. It's up to you. The point is to share the love of Christ and the joy of the season with somebody who needs to know they are loved. Take a few minutes to talk about what you and your family could do this Christmas.

PUTTING IT INTO PRACTICE

1. Read pages 38 – 83 in *The Purpose of Christmas* this week. Be prepared to share your thoughts and insights with the group in your next session.

2. Congratulations if you have already started planning your group's Christmas party. For those of you who haven't decided when you will host your party, it's not too late. Simply ask the "party person" of your group to coordinate with the rest. Even if it's a very simple get-together for dessert or a Christmas ornament/cookie making party, you don't want to miss out on this. It could become a new holiday tradition for you.

PRAYER DIRECTION

Following you will find two sections, one for personal prayer and one for group prayer requests. Take a few minutes to write a personal prayer based on today's session and what you're most thankful about. Then write down a few of the group prayer requests before you pray together.

Personal Prayer

Father, today I learned … _____

_____

_____

_____

_____

_____

Thank you, Lord, for … _____

_____

_____

_____

_____

_____

Group Prayer

Name   Request

_____   _____

_____   _____

_____   _____

_____   _____

_____   _____

_____   _____

_____   _____

Now turn the page for this week's Daily Christmas Prayer Journal.

DAILY CHRISTMAS PRAYER JOURNAL

Teach me, Lord …   *December 8*

_____

_____

_____

_____

_____

Lord, my life has meaning because …   *December 9*

_____

_____

_____

_____

_____

God, please give me the heart to …   *December 10*

_____

_____

_____

_____

_____

Jesus, I will always remember ...   *December 11*

_____

_____

_____

_____

Father, the purpose of my life is to ...   *December 12*

_____

_____

_____

_____

Lord, help me overcome ...   *December 13*

_____

_____

_____

_____

Today, Lord, I just want to tell you ...   *December 14*

_____

_____

_____

_____

SESSION THREE

A Time for Reconciliation

CATCHING UP

1. If you read the assigned pages (38–83) in *The Purpose of Christmas* this week, share something that was particularly meaningful to you.

2. In our last session, we learned that we are saved *from* sin, *for* God's purpose, and *by* God's grace. How did that shape your perspective this week?

KEY VERSE

God ... reconciled us to himself through Christ and gave us the <u>*ministry*</u> *of reconciliation.... And he has committed to us the* <u>*message*</u> *of reconciliation. We are therefore Christ's ambassadors.*

2 Corinthians 5:18–20 NIV (emphasis added)

Watch the Session Three video now and fill in the blanks in the outline on pages 37–39. Refer back to the outline during your discussion time.

A TIME FOR RECONCILIATION

God has three purposes for Christmas, and we discover those purposes in the announcement the angel made at the birth of Jesus Christ.

The first purpose of Christmas is celebration — *"I bring you good news of great joy that will be for all the people."*

The second purpose of Christmas is salvation — *"For unto you is born this day a Savior who is Christ the Lord."*

The third purpose of Christmas is found in this statement —

Glory to God in the highest, and on earth peace, good will toward men. (Luke 2:14 KJV)

The third purpose of Christmas is _____.

What is reconciliation? Reconciliation is when a broken relationship is restored. Reconciliation is peace on earth, good will toward men.

There will never be peace in the world until there is peace in nations. There will never be peace in nations until there is peace in communities. There will never be peace in communities until there is peace in families. There will never be peace in families until there is peace in individuals. There will never be peace in individuals until we invite the Prince of Peace to reign in our hearts. Jesus is the Prince of Peace.

For to us a child is born, to us a son is given ... and he will be called Prince of Peace. (Isaiah 9:6 NIV)

Three Kinds of Peace

1. Peace _____ **is** _____ **peace.**

If you're trying to live your life without God, then you're at war with God and you need a peace treaty.

> *Now that we have been put right with God through faith, we have peace with God through our Lord Jesus Christ. (Romans 5:1 TEV)*

How do you make peace with God? You don't do it by promising to be good. You don't do it by being perfect. You can't. You don't do it by never sinning. You will. You make peace, the Bible says, by faith — faith in God's grace.

> *For by grace you have been saved through faith. And this is not your own doing; it is the gift of God. (Ephesians 2:8 ESV)*

2. The peace _____ is _____ peace.

The peace *of* God happens in your heart when you've made peace *with* God.

> *Don't worry about anything; instead pray about everything. (Philippians 4:6 NLT)*

You've got two choices in life. In every circumstance, you can pray or panic. You can worship or worry. If you prayed as much as you worry, you'd have a whole lot less to worry about.

> *6Pray about everything. Tell God what you need, and thank him for all he has done. 7If you do this, you will experience God's peace, which is far more wonderful than the human mind can understand. His peace will guard your hearts and minds as you live in Christ Jesus. (Philippians 4:6–7 NLT)*

3. Peace _____ **is** _____ **peace.**

> [18]*God … reconciled us to himself through Christ and gave us the* <u>*ministry*</u> *of reconciliation.…* [19]*And he has committed to us the* <u>*message*</u> *of reconciliation.* [20]*We are therefore Christ's ambassadors.* (2 Corinthians 5:18–20 NIV, emphasis added)

In other words, God has given us both a ministry and a message … and it's reconciliation — helping people find peace with God and peace with each other.

> *"Blessed are the peacemakers, for they shall be called the children of God." (Matthew 5:9 KJV)*

The greatest need in our nation and in our world is reconciliation. It's the message of Christmas: Peace on earth, good will toward men.

Who do you need to rebuild a broken relationship with this Christmas? Who do you need to reconcile with? You're going to have to let Jesus Christ fill you with his love so you can love other people the way he does. And you're going to have to let him fill you with his forgiveness. Until you feel truly forgiven, you don't have the ability to forgive others.

> *It makes no difference who you are or where you're from. If you want God, and you're ready to do as he says, the door is open. (Acts 10:35 MSG)*

If you just prayed with Pastor Rick to invite Jesus Christ into your life, he would love to hear from you. You can send Pastor Rick an email at *pastorrick@saddleback.com*.

DISCOVERY QUESTIONS

1. Pastor Rick talked about three kinds of peace: peace *with* God; the peace *of* God; peace *with* others. In which of these areas do you need to invite the Prince of Peace to reign this Christmas?

2. In every circumstance, you can pray or panic, you can worship or worry. But the Bible is clear on God's perspective about difficulties: *"Don't worry about anything; instead pray about everything"* (Philippians 4:6 NLT). Briefly share about a time when you experienced the peace of God by turning from panic to prayer.

3. Pastor Rick said, "You're going to have to let Jesus Christ fill you with his love and forgiveness so you can love and forgive other people the way he does." Without mentioning names or details, think of the person who came to mind when Rick talked about reconciling a relationship. What step can you take toward love and forgiveness?

4. A peacemaker is a person who builds people up and compliments them more than he criticizes. A peacemaker loves people the way Jesus does. How can you be a peacemaker with a family member, neighbor, friend, or coworker this Christmas?

5. Jesus Christ is God's Christmas gift to you. Have you opened that gift and made peace with God? If so, would two or three of you like to tell the group how you accepted that gift? If you have not accepted God's gift, feel free to share where you are in your spiritual journey.

LIVING ON PURPOSE: WORSHIP

You have just completed the entire study on *The Purpose of Christmas*. What gift do you want to give God this Christmas? What gift are you grateful for? As an act of worship to God, why not dedicate this holiday season to him?

One practical way you can do this is to take a moment on Christmas Eve to ask everyone in your family to share one thing they thank God for this last year and one thing they want to surrender this next year. This single idea could deepen your relationship with God and with your entire family, and it could become a new Christmas tradition in your home.

Reflect on the gifts God has given you, such as friends, children, new relationships, your church, good health, provision, etc. Then ask yourself, *What gift can I give back to God as an act of worship and gratitude?* This could include your heart, your career, your time, your fears, your future, etc. Write your thoughts in the gift boxes on page 42. Then have a few people share with the group what they wrote.

Lord, thank you for giving me ...

Lord, I am giving you ...

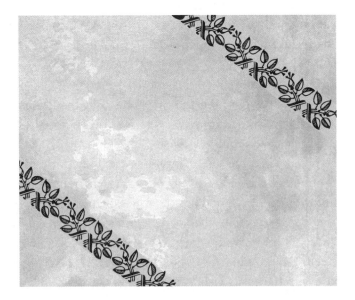

PUTTING IT INTO PRACTICE

1. Read pages 84 – 117 in *The Purpose of Christmas* this week. Hopefully you have found this book helpful in your understanding of the true meaning of Christmas. Why not give a copy of *The Purpose of Christmas* to a few of your family and friends. Hopefully they too can discover the true power and purpose of the Christmas season.

2. Do you need to start rebuilding a broken relationship this Christmas? Perhaps this can be one of your "gifts" to Jesus. Reconciliation can be difficult; sometimes it is a real sacrifice. But it is necessary. The Bible says:

   [17]Do not repay anyone evil for evil. Be careful to do what is right in the eyes of everybody. [18]If it is possible, as far as it depends on you, live at peace with everyone. [19]Do not take revenge, my friends, but leave room for God's wrath, for it is written: "It is mine to avenge; I will repay," says the Lord. [20]On the contrary: "If your enemy is hungry, feed him; if he is thirsty, give him something to drink. In doing this, you will heap burning coals on his head." [21]Do not be overcome by evil, but overcome evil with good. (Romans 12:17 – 21 NIV)

   Here's a first step toward reconciliation: Regardless of who is at fault, ask God every day to bless that person. Ask God to give you the grace to forgive, the courage to seek forgiveness, and the wisdom to know what he wants you to do. Then ask somebody to be your spiritual partner in this matter so they can help you follow through on your commitment. (See page 56 in the Frequently Asked Questions section of this study guide for more information on spiritual partners.)

PRAYER DIRECTION

Below you will find two sections, one for personal prayer and one for group prayer requests. Take a few minutes to write a personal prayer based on today's lesson and what you're most thankful for. Then write down a few of the group prayer requests before you pray together.

Personal Prayer

Father, today I learned ... _____

_____

_____

_____

_____

_____

Thank you, Lord, for ... _____

_____

_____

_____

_____

_____

Group Prayer

Name   Request

_____   _____

_____   _____

_____   _____

_____   _____

_____   _____

_____   _____

_____   _____

Now turn the page for this week's Daily Christmas Prayer Journal. Note that there's an extra page (page 48) in this journal to get you all the way to Christmas Day.

DAILY CHRISTMAS PRAYER JOURNAL

Jesus, thank you for saving me from ...   *December 15*

_____

_____

_____

_____

_____

Father, I choose to give you ...   *December 16*

_____

_____

_____

_____

_____

Lord, where I really need your touch is ...   *December 17*

_____

_____

_____

_____

_____

Lord, I will never forget …   *December 18*

_____

_____

_____

_____

Please, Lord, help me reconcile with …   *December 19*

_____

_____

_____

_____

God, I thank you today for …   *December 20*

_____

_____

_____

_____

Lord, help me to remember that …   *December 21*

_____

_____

_____

_____

Jesus, I'm asking you to help my friend ...   *December 22*

_____

_____

_____

_____

Lord, my heart yearns for ...   *December 23*

_____

_____

_____

_____

Jesus, above all else, I want you to know ...   *December 24*

_____

_____

_____

_____

Happy birthday, Jesus ...   *December 25*

_____

_____

_____

_____

Group
Resources

Helps for Hosts

Top Ten Ideas for New Group Hosts

Congratulations! As the host of your small group, you have responded to the call to help shepherd Jesus' flock. Few other tasks in the family of God surpass the contribution you will be making. As you prepare to facilitate your group, whether it is one session or the entire series, here are a few thoughts to keep in mind.

Remember you are not alone. God knows everything about you, and he knew you would be asked to facilitate your group. Even though you may not feel ready, this is common for all good hosts. God promises, *"I will never leave you; I will never abandon you"* (Hebrews 13:5 TEV). Whether you are facilitating for one evening, several weeks, or a lifetime, you will be blessed as you serve.

1. **Don't try to do it alone.** Pray right now for God to help you build a healthy team. If you can enlist a cohost to help you shepherd the group, you will find your experience much richer. This is your chance to involve as many people as you can in building a healthy group. All you have to do is ask people to help. You'll be surprised at the response.

2. **Be friendly and be yourself.** God wants to use your unique gifts and temperament. Be sure to greet people at the door with a big smile. This can set the mood for the whole gathering. Remember, they are taking as big a step to show up at your house as you are to host this group! Don't try to do things exactly like another host; do them in a way that fits you. Admit when you don't have an answer and apologize when you make a mistake. Your group will love you for it and you'll sleep better at night.

3. **Prepare for your meeting ahead of time.** Review the session and write down your responses to each question. Pay special attention to exercises that ask group members to do something other than engage in discussion. These exercises

will help your group live what the Bible teaches, not just talk about it. Be sure you understand how an exercise works. If the exercise employs one of the items in the Group Resources section (such as the Group Guidelines), be sure to look over that item so you'll know how it works.

4. **Pray for your group members by name.** Before your group arrives, take a few moments and pray for each member by name. You may want to review the prayer list at least once a week. Ask God to use your time together to touch the heart of every person in your group. Expect God to direct you to whomever he wants you to encourage or challenge in a special way. If you listen, God will surely lead.

5. **When you ask a question, be patient.** Someone will eventually respond. Sometimes people need a moment or two of silence to think about the question. If silence doesn't bother you, it won't bother anyone else. After someone responds, affirm the response with a simple "thanks" or "great answer." Then ask, "How about somebody else?" or "Would someone who hasn't shared like to add anything?" Be sensitive to new people or reluctant members who aren't ready to say, pray, or do anything. If you give them a safe setting, they will blossom over time. If someone in your group is a "wallflower" who sits silently through every session, consider talking to them privately and encouraging them to participate. Let them know how important they are to you — that they are loved and appreciated — and that the group would value their input. Remember, still water often runs deep.

6. **Provide transitions between questions.** Ask if anyone would like to read the paragraph or Bible passage. Don't call on anyone, but ask for a volunteer, and then be patient until someone begins. Be sure to thank the person who reads aloud.

7. **Break into smaller groups occasionally.** With a greater opportunity to talk in a small circle, people will connect more with the study, apply more quickly what they're learning, and ultimately get more out of their small group experience. A small circle also encourages a quiet person to participate and tends to minimize the effects of a more vocal or dominant member.

8. **Small circles are also helpful during prayer time.** People who are unaccustomed to praying aloud will feel more comfortable trying it with just two or three others. Also, prayer requests won't take as much time, so circles will have more time to actually pray. When you gather back with the whole group, you can have one person from each circle briefly update everyone on the prayer requests from their subgroups. The other great aspect of subgrouping is that it fosters leadership development. As you ask people in the group to facilitate discussion or lead a prayer circle, it gives them a small leadership step that can build their confidence.

9. **Rotate facilitators occasionally.** You may be perfectly capable of hosting each time, but you will help others grow in their faith and gifts if you give them opportunities to host the group.

10. **One final challenge**. Before your first opportunity to lead, read each of the six Scripture passages that follow as a devotional exercise to help prepare you with a shepherd's heart. Trust us on this one. If you do this, you will be more than ready for your first meeting.

Matthew 9:36 – 38 (NIV)

³⁶*When Jesus saw the crowds, he had compassion on them, because they were harassed and helpless, like sheep without a shepherd.* ³⁷*Then he said to his disciples, "The harvest is plentiful but the workers are few.* ³⁸*Ask the Lord of the harvest, therefore, to send out workers into his harvest field."*

John 10:14 – 15 (NIV)

¹⁴*I am the good shepherd; I know my sheep and my sheep know me —* ¹⁵*just as the Father knows me and I know the Father — and I lay down my life for the sheep.*

1 Peter 5:2 – 4 (NIV)

²*Be shepherds of God's flock that is under your care, serving as overseers — not because you must, but because you are willing, as God wants you to be; not greedy for money, but eager to serve;* ³*not lording it over those entrusted to you, but being examples to the flock.* ⁴*And when the Chief Shepherd appears, you will receive the crown of glory that will never fade away.*

Philippians 2:1 – 5 (NIV)

¹*If you have any encouragement from being united with Christ, if any comfort from his love, if any fellowship with the Spirit, if any tenderness and compassion,* ²*then make my joy complete by being like-minded, having the same love, being one in spirit and purpose.* ³*Do nothing out of selfish ambition or vain conceit, but in humility consider others better than yourselves.* ⁴*Each of you should look not only to your own interests, but also to the interests of others.* ⁵*Your attitude should be the same as that of Jesus Christ.*

Hebrews 10:23 – 25 (NIV)

[23]Let us hold unswervingly to the hope we profess, for he who promised is faithful. [24]And let us consider how we may spur one another on toward love and good deeds. [25]Let us not give up meeting together, as some are in the habit of doing, but let us encourage one another — and all the more as you see the Day approaching.

1 Thessalonians 2:7 – 8, 11 – 12 (NIV)

[7]... but we were gentle among you, like a mother caring for her little children. [8]We loved you so much that we were delighted to share with you not only the gospel of God but our lives as well, because you had become so dear to us....[11]For you know that we dealt with each of you as a father deals with his own children, [12]encouraging, comforting and urging you to live lives worthy of God, who calls you into his kingdom and glory.

FREQUENTLY ASKED QUESTIONS

How long will this group meet?

The Purpose of Christmas is three sessions long. In your final session, each group member may decide if he or she desires to continue on for another study. At that time you may also want to do some informal evaluation, discuss your group guidelines, and decide which study you want to do next. We recommend you visit our website at *www.saddlebackresources. com* for more video-based small group studies.

Who is the host?

The host is the person who coordinates and facilitates your group meetings. In addition to a host, we encourage you to select one or more group members to lead your group discussions. Several other responsibilities can be rotated, including refreshments, prayer requests, worship, or keeping up with those who miss a meeting. Shared ownership in the group helps everybody grow.

Where do we find new group members?

Recruiting new members can be a challenge for groups, especially new groups with just a few people, or existing groups that lose a few people along the way. We encourage you to use the Circles of Life diagram on page 59 of this study guide to brainstorm a list of people from your workplace, church, school, neighborhood, family, and so on. Then pray for the people on each member's list. Allow each member to invite several people from their list. Some groups fear that newcomers will interrupt the intimacy that members have built over time. However, groups that welcome newcomers generally gain strength with the infusion of new blood. Remember, the next person you add just might become a friend for eternity. Logistically, groups find different ways to add members. Some groups remain permanently open, while others choose to open periodically, such as at the beginning or end of a study. If your group becomes too large for easy, face-to-face conversations, you can subgroup, forming a second discussion group in another room.

How do we handle the child care needs in our group?

Child care needs must be handled very carefully. This is a sensitive issue. We suggest you seek creative solutions as a group. One common solution is to have the adults meet in the living room and share the cost of a babysitter (or two) who can be with the kids in another part of the house. Another popular option is to have one home for the kids and a second home (close by) for the adults. If desired, the adults could rotate the responsibility of providing a lesson for the kids. This last option is great with school-age kids and can be a huge blessing to families.

What is a spiritual partner?

Spiritual health, like physical health, is often easier to maintain when you are working out with a partner. As you "work out" what God is working in you, sometimes you need someone to encourage you and help keep you on target. Prayerfully consider which member of your group you might ask to become your spiritual partner. We recommend that men partner with men, women with women, or spouse with spouse. Commit to pray for each other for the duration of this study. Check in throughout the week by phone, or perhaps over coffee, to see what each of you is learning and how you can pray for one another.

GROUP GUIDELINES

It's a good idea for every group to put words to their shared values, expectations, and commitments. Such guidelines will help you avoid unspoken agendas and unmet expectations. We recommend you discuss your guidelines during Session One in order to lay the foundation for a healthy group experience. Feel free to modify anything that does not work for your group.

We agree to the following values:

- **Clear Purpose:** To grow healthy spiritual lives by building a healthy small group community.
- **Group Attendance:** To give priority to the group meeting (call if I am absent or late).
- **Safe Environment:** To create a safe place where people can be heard and feel loved (no quick answers, snap judgments, or simple fixes).
- **Be Confidential:** To keep anything that is shared strictly confidential and within the group.
- **Conflict Resolution:** To avoid gossip and to immediately resolve any concerns by following the principles of Matthew 18:15 – 17.
- **Spiritual Health:** To give group members permission to speak into my life and help me live a healthy, balanced spiritual life that is pleasing to God.
- **Limit Our Freedom**: To limit our freedom by not serving or consuming alcohol during small group meetings or events so as to avoid causing a weaker brother or sister to stumble (1 Corinthians 8:1 – 13; Romans 14:19 – 21).
- **Welcome Newcomers:** To invite friends who might benefit from this study, and warmly welcome newcomers.

- **Building Relationships:** To get to know the other members of the group and pray for them regularly.
- **Other:** _____

   _____

   _____

We have also discussed and agree on the following items:

- **Child care:** _____
- **Starting time:** _____
- **Ending time:** _____

If you haven't already done so, take a few minutes to fill out the Small Group Calendar on page 60.

CIRCLES OF LIFE — SMALL GROUP CONNECTIONS

Discover Who You Can Connect in Community

Use this chart to help carry out one of the values in the group guidelines, to "Welcome newcomers."

Then He said to them, "Follow Me, and I will make you fishers of men." (Matthew 4:19 NKJV)

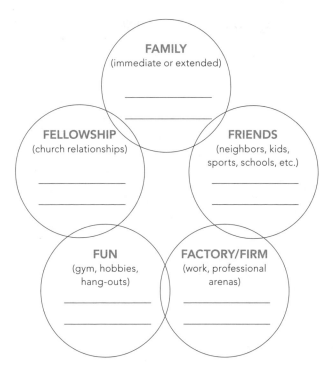

Follow this simple three-step process:

1. List one or two people in each circle.
2. Prayerfully select one person or couple from your list and tell your group about them.
3. Give them a call and invite them to your next meeting. Over 50 percent of those invited to a small group say, "Yes!"

SMALL GROUP CALENDAR

Healthy groups share responsibilities and group ownership. It might take some time for this to develop. Shared ownership ensures that responsibility for the group doesn't fall to one person. Use the calendar to keep track of social events, mission projects, birthdays, or days off. Complete this calendar at your first or second meeting. Planning ahead will increase attendance and shared ownership of the group.

DATE	LESSON	FACILITATOR	SNACK OR MEAL
5/4	Session 2	Chris and Amy	Phil and Karen

ANSWER KEY

Session One: A Time for Celebration

The first purpose of Christmas is <u>celebration</u>.
1. God *loves* you.
2. God is *with* you.
3. God is *for* you.

Session Two: A Time for Salvation

The second purpose of Christmas is <u>salvation</u>.
1. Jesus came to save you *from* <u>sin</u>.
2. Jesus came to save you *for* a <u>purpose</u>.
3. Jesus came to save you *by* his <u>grace</u>.
<u>God's</u>
<u>R</u>iches
<u>At</u>
<u>Christ's</u>
<u>Ex</u>pense

Session Three: A Time for Reconciliation

The third purpose of Christmas is <u>reconciliation</u>.
1. Peace <u>with God</u> is <u>spiritual</u> peace.
2. The peace <u>of God</u> is <u>emotional</u> peace.
3. Peace <u>with others</u> is <u>relational</u> peace.

Foundations: 11 Core Truths to Build Your Life On

Taught by Tom Holladay and Kay Warren

Foundations is a series of 11 four-week video studies covering the most important, foundational doctrines of the Christian faith. Study topics include:

The Bible—This study focuses on where the Bible came from, why it can be trusted, and how it can change your life.

DVD Study Guide: 978-0-310-27670-8
DVD: 978-0-310-27669-2

God—This study focuses not just on facts about God, but on how to know God himself in a more powerful and personal way.

DVD Study Guide: 978-0-310-27672-2
DVD: 978-0-310-27671-5

Jesus—As we look at what the Bible says about the person of Christ, we do so as people who are developing a lifelong relationship with Jesus.

DVD Study Guide: 978-0-310-27674-6
DVD: 978-0-310-27673-9

The Holy Spirit—This study focuses on the person, the presence, and the power of the Holy Spirit, and how you can be filled with the Holy Spirit on a daily basis.

DVD Study Guide: 978-0-310-27676-0
DVD: 978-0-310-27675-3

Creation—Each of us was personally created by a loving God. This study does not shy away from the great scientific and theological arguments that surround the creation/evolution debate. However, you will find the goal of this study is deepening your awareness of God as your Creator.

DVD Study Guide: 978-0-310-27678-4
DVD: 978-0-310-27677-7

Pick up a copy today at your favorite bookstore!

ZONDERVAN®
.com

Salvation—This study focuses on God's solution to man's need for salvation, what Jesus Christ did for us on the cross, and the assurance and security of God's love and provision for eternity.

DVD Study Guide: 978-0-310-27682-1
DVD: 978-0-310-27679-1

Sanctification—This study focuses on the two natures of the Christian. We'll see the difference between grace and law, and how these two things work in our lives.

DVD Study Guide: 978-0-310-27684-5
DVD: 978-0-310-27683-8

Good and Evil—Why do bad things happen to good people? Through this study we'll see how and why God continues to allow evil to exist. The ultimate goal is to build up our faith and relationship with God as we wrestle with these difficult questions.

DVD Study Guide: 978-0-310-27687-6
DVD: 978-0-310-27686-9

The Afterlife—The Bible does not answer all the questions we have about what happens to us after we die; however, this study deals with what the Bible does tell us. This important study gives us hope and helps us move from a focus on the here and now to a focus on eternity.

DVD Study Guide: 978-0-310-27689-0
DVD: 978-0-310-27688-3

The Church—This study focuses on the birth of the church, the nature of the church, and the mission of the church.

DVD Study Guide: 978-0-310-27692-0
DVD: 978-0-310-27691-3

The Second Coming—This study addresses both the hope and the uncertainties surrounding the second coming of Jesus Christ.

DVD Study Guide: 978-0-310-27695-1
DVD: 978-0-310-27693-7

Pick up a copy today at your favorite bookstore!

The Purpose Driven® Life
A six-session video-based study for groups or individuals

Embark on a journey of discovery with this video-based study taught by Rick Warren. In it you will discover the answer to life's most fundamental question: "What on earth am I here for?"

And here's a clue to the answer: "It's not about you . . . You were created by God and for God, and until you understand that, life will never make sense. It is only in God that we discover our origin, our identity, our meaning, our purpose, our significance, and our destiny."

Whether you experience this adventure with a small group or on your own, this six-session, video-based study will change your life.

DVD Study Guide: 978-0-310-27866-5
DVD: 978-0-310-27864-1

Be sure to combine this study with your reading of the bestselling book, *The Purpose Driven® Life,* to give you or your small group the opportunity to discuss the implications and applications of living the life God created you to live.

Hardcover, Jacketed: 978-0-310-20571-5
Softcover: 978-0-310-27699-9

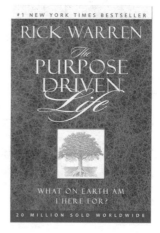

Pick up a copy today at your favorite bookstore!

HarperChristian Resources